BURNOUT PROOF

How To Establish Boundaries To Avoid The Negativity Of Stress

BREAKFAST LEADERSHIP, INC.

Burnout Proof: How To Establish Boundaries
To Avoid The Negativity Of Stress

ISN: 978-1-64746-560-5 (Paperback)
ISBN:: 978-1-64746-561-2 (Hardback)
ISBN: 978-1-64746-562-9 (Ebook)
LCCN: 2020920216

To Dad.

CONTENTS

INTRODUCTION

Ever notice* how when you're focused on something, you start noticing it all the time? For example, let's say you buy a car. Next thing you know, you notice a bazillion cars just like yours on the road. (Frustrating if you want to be the only person in town who has that vehicle.) Well, I notice burnout. Burned-out people, burned-out departments, burned-out families, and so on. We are a stressed society, and our millennial population seems to be as attracted to burnout as they are rumored to be addicted to avocado toast. (I kid, I kid: as a Gen Xer, I applaud the younger generation for eating healthier than my generation has.)

(Note: Whenever I see the phrase "Ever notice . . . ", `` I hear it in Andy Rooney's voice. For people born after 1980, Andy Rooney used to have a segment on 60 Minutes, and he often led with the words, "Ever notice . . . " when he was observing a situation in life. By the way, 60 Minutes is a TV news show on CBS. That's a television network. Yes, there are other networks besides Netflix.)

We see more and more stories on burnout in mainstream media (or, as us old people call it, "Network TV"). Burnout is mainstream—and that stream is growing to a river, a lake, a whole damn ocean. People of all walks of life, genders, and races, are burning out faster than any other time in recorded history. Why? Oh, my friend, that is a loaded question, and I will attempt to answer it in this book. To quote a colleague of mine that works in the field of law, the short answer is, "It depends." (Kate should get that phrase trademarked.) Why people burn out depends on what led to their burned-out state.

Burnout doesn't happen overnight. You won't wake up tomorrow morning and say, "Dang, I caught some burnout last night." Burnout slowly builds up—often innocently—based on your behaviors, habits, and choices. As I've worked with a variety of people who have experienced burnout, including myself, I've noticed some patterns. The common reasons people burn out are:

People- Pleasing
Lack of Boundaries
Improper Diet
Lack of Exercise
Lack of Quality Sleep (You need seven hours or more, boss!)
Lack of Self- Confidence
Past Traumas and/or PTSD
Workplace Issues (Workload, culture—lions, tigers, and bears, oh my!)
Lack of (Perceived) Control
Lack of Community (Do you know your neighbor's name?)
Social Media (Which should be called anti-social media)
 Mismatched Values With Loved Ones or Your Workplace Culture

I'll dive into each of those items throughout the book. As with all things in life, burnout may be caused by a combination of things. The key is to understand if you do have burnout—and if you do, how to recover from it and prevent it from happening again.

"What you resist, persists."
—Attributed to Carl Jung

CHAPTER 1
WHAT IS BURNOUT?

Burnout is a state of emotional, physical, and mental exhaustion caused by excessive and prolonged stress. It occurs when you feel overwhelmed, emotionally drained, and unable to meet constant demands. Burnout has been front and center (centre in Canada) in the cultural conversation—and even the intercultural conversation, as we are experiencing a burnout epidemic across the planet. Every industry, every role, every age and gender is experiencing burnout at an alarming rate.

Burnout is not a new term. Dr. Herbert Freudenberger published Burnout: The High Cost of High Achievement back in 1980. That's forty years ago—80s music, 90s grunge, the dot.com bubble, 9/11, the Cubs' World Series win, and Trump becoming president have all occurred since Dr. Freudenberger's book was released. Yet burnout persists, and has expanded, despite Dr. Fruedenberger's warnings. In his book, this is how Freudenberger defines the term burnout:

Burn-out: To deplete oneself. To exhaust one's physical and men-tal resources. To wear oneself out by excessively striving to reach some unrealistic expectations imposed by one self or by the values of society.

Every generation struggles with burnout. Every kind of person struggles with burnout: single parents, married parents, children, grandparents, front- line staff, and CEOs. The largest living generation at the time of this book is Gen Y (aka millennials). Much has been written about this generation, and avocado toast jokes aside, Gen Y is a generation in search of itself. Unrealistic expectations of life often ignite burnout. Millennials often say, "I should have a house by now," or " Why do I have so much student loan debt?" Market conditions have put home ownership out of reach for many people across the globe, especially in large metropolitan areas. It's only getting worse. Student loan debt is a major burden to millennials, and according to my colleague Steve Olsher, 87 percent of college graduates do not work in their field of study five years after graduating. (This stat is getting worse, and I agree with Mr. Bold on his stance that going to college is the worst financial decision you can make. Take out loans, sure, but invest them and go learn a trade that's actually in demand.)

Millennials expect the perfect job, the perfect relationship, the house with the picket fence, and they expect it by age twenty-five. Guess what? Not bloody likely to happen, Gen Y. When you expect so many external factors to make you happy, and those factors do not come to you like you want or expect, you're setting yourself up for failure, high stress, and burnout.

You're choosing to be burned out. I know that stings, and you don't believe me. Fine, don't believe me. I used to think like you do, but I learned a very hard and devastating lesson. (More on that later on.)

79 Percent of People Are Stressed 24/7

As mentioned earlier, burnout is impacting every role in every industry, however one profession's burnout is having a huge impact on society, and if left unaddressed, will cause great harm to society as our population gets older. In less than twenty years, the population over age sixty-five will double, and the number of people living past ninety will triple. That's a lot of senior discounts! Joking aside, though, seniors tend to be the largest users of the healthcare system, and our trusted doctors are struggling horribly with burnout.

According to Annals of Internal Medicine, physician burnout costs the healthcare system approximately $4.6 billion (yes, billion with a B) every year, due to turnover, reduced productivity and other burnout-related factors.

Imagine what $4.6 billion could do if it weren't lost on physicians burning out—healthcare for more people, increased access to care, real investments in mental health (a huge component of burnout), and research. However, billions are lost due to the high stress and resultant burnout of our healthcare providers are experiencing.

Physician suicide is the highest of any profession. The migration from paper charts to electronic health records (EHRs or EMRs—Electronic Medical Records—for short) has caused a huge increase in the number of hours that physicians and clinicians work, and with increased compliance and reporting that is expected of physicians, their patient billings (aka dollars) are decreasing. Working more hours for less pay? Sounds awesome—sign me up!

In Jeffrey Pfeffer's book Dying for a Paycheck, Jeffrey states that 61 percent of employees said workplace stress had made them sick, and 7 percent said they had actually been hospitalized because of stress. Job stress costs US employers more than $300 billion annually and may cause 120,000 excess deaths each year. In China, 1 million people a year may be dying from overwork. People are literally dying for a paycheck.

Suddenly, homelessness or living in a shelter sounds like a better option. Think about it : a roof over your head, three square meals a day, no time clock, no midnight emails from your incompetent boss, and no more constant strain, backstabbing and politics. Yes, you have to brave the elements if you can't get into a shelter, but c'mon, the bullshit that employers are putting employees through across the globe has gotten out of hand! You have to admit that homelessness is at least a little appealing.

We often pick the wrong jobs because we focus on the money alone. We never ask what hours we'll really be expected to work. Ask your next interviewer, "Will my manager often text or email me after hours ?" If they say yes, stand up, thank the interviewer, and run as fast as you can out of that shit hole of an establishment.

The challenges workers face today resemble the way workplaces were before the union movement in the 1900s . . . food for thought.

BOUNDARIES

Burnout is an epidemic. We're seeing it all throughout our country and across the planet. People are leaving their jobs or going long-term on leave because they simply can't take it anymore.

A while back, I posted an image on Instagram that turned the word burnout into an acronym. The letter B was for boundaries. I think a key to dealing with your burnout is boundaries. If you don't have boundaries, you're going to burn out; it's inevitable. Your self-worth and your self-care get impacted when you don't have boundaries in your life.

When they hear the word boundaries, a lot of people think of border walls, boundaries around a sports field, or something along those lines. Personal boundaries are important. You have to take care of yourself first. We've all heard the analogy of putting on your oxygen mask first if you're an airplane crash. (Hopefully you never experience that, because it's quite traumatic for people who have.) You're on an airplane, masks drop, and everyone starts freaking out—but you have to shift out of that panic state and you have to take care of yourself.

In all aspects of your life, you have to take care of yourself, so boundaries are important. How do you implement boundaries in your life if you don't have them already? Just like anything, you have to implement them slowly, and you have to see what works and what doesn't.

Saying no is a boundary. Don't overcommit yourself. Don't spend so much time giving to others that you don't take care of yourself. You can't serve if you're empty. Unfortunately, many of us find ourselves constantly giving and giving, and we're not giving to ourselves.

I understand that. I get it. I am a reformed people pleaser, and people pleasers want to help others. And sometimes when you can't give people what they want when they want it, they get angry. If you're anti-confrontational, you take that personally. Remember, they're projecting their wants and their desires, and what's an emergency to them may not be an emergency to you. You want to help people when you can. Ultimately it boils down helping yourself first. If you don't do that, you're not going to help anybody (at least, not in the way that you'd want to).

UNHAPPY

In the BURNOUT acronym, the letter U is for unhappy. When you're burned out, you're not happy with yourself. You're not happy with life. You're not happy about anything. You may be upset. You may be mad. You're numb. You don't sleep well. You're not eating well. You're not doing anything well. Life is just overwhelming to you, to the point where even little inconveniences seem like major catastrophes in your life.

If that's going on with you, it's a warning sign that you need to address something. When I had my burnout, I was distant from life. Things that I used to enjoy, things that brought me fulfillment, no longer did. This isn't normal. Little things shouldn't bug you. When I created my BURNOUT acronym, it was summertime 2019 in North America, and it seemed a lot of people were on edge. Summertime is supposed to be a time of relaxation, sitting outside on patios, enjoying the nice weather. If you're in a climate that doesn't have warm weather year-round, summer is a good time to reconnect with people by experiencing things together: to go to a baseball game, go out to eat, find restaurants, go to plays, concerts, and outdoor venues. All of these things are all over the place.

If you're not partaking in those things because you're too tired, don't have the energy, or have no time, that's a warning sign. If you're unhappy with your life and you're not doing the things that bring you joy and happiness, your burnout is going to get worse, and you'll start experiencing other physical and mental issues. Eventually, the energy your body needs to maintain itself won't be there to repair the damage you're doing to it. That's why your sleep is garbage. That's why your energy levels are low. That's why the high-octane coffee isn't doing what it used to do. It's because you're burned out and you're not enjoying life and you're unhappy. And you can address this, but you have to be willing and able to do it.

RHYTHM

We're up to the letter R, which stands for rhythm. Our lives are about harmony and rhythm. When you're burned out, you're out of rhythm. In our lives, we build up habits, routines, and a variety of different things. When you're out of rhythm, those things become harder to do (or you skip them). I often see that burned-out people skip the things they enjoy doing because they don't have time . . . or at least they think they don't have time.

You've got twenty-four hours a day, seven days a week, three hundred sixty-five days a year. If it's a leap year, you get a bonus day. (Pro tip: take a vacation day on leap day. Use that day as a day of reflection. Enjoy yourself. Do whatever you want.)

When your life is not in rhythm, everything becomes harder, even getting out of bed or going to the gym or meeting up with people. When you're out of rhythm, it's as if you're not quite driving on the road. You're driving on the shoulder. You're running over things. You're hearing clunks in your car. Everything is a mess—and it's because you're not taking care of yourself.

If you're not in alignment, again, your body is going to compensate for the problems that you're dealing with. Your body needs energy to repair the damage that you do to it on a daily basis, but that energy won't be there, because it'll be used to address your out- of- rhythm situation.

The key is to get back into rhythm. You need to return to your true self, align to your true north. And to do that, you need to get to come to grips with the fact that there's something wrong. You're out of alignment. There's something going on that has led you to this burned-out state. It doesn't cure itself.

Even taking a couple weeks vacation to get away from everything won't fix it: after all, you should want a life that you don't have to take a vacation to get away from. When you get back from vacation, guess what? You have two weeks of work on top of your normal workload. That's why you hear people grumbling all the time about going back to work. It's because their workloads are not manageable. And that's a systemic problem. We're being asked to do too much, and oftentimes, we don't have enough resources to do it. That's the reality of things.

The key is to find alignment with what you can do and specialize in the things that only you can do. That's a hard conversation with your employers. That's a hard conversation with your family, your friends, your partner, your kids, everybody. You can only do so much. You're not going to be able to get everything done. (That's a spoiler alert.) There's no shortage of work, which is a good thing, because it means there are things for us to do. The key is to get into rhythm with the things we need to do.

NEGLECT

Next up in the BURNOUT acronym is the letter N for neglect. You're neglecting your self-care. Oh, a reminder: burnout doesn't happen overnight; it takes time. When we enter that burnout arena, we start neglecting our self-care. What do I mean by self-care? You hear that phrase a lot, but many people don't understand what it means.

Self-care means making sure that you're taking care of yourself: physically, mentally, spiritually and any other -ly that you can come up with. You need to take care of yourself. You need to eat well—that doesn't mean that you're skipping fast food every day, but you should probably cut down. When I had my burn out, my "nutrition plan" was ordering something through a speaker, driving around the corner, and getting a brown paper bag. I was working crazy hours and not sitting down and eating, so I basically consumed fast food for breakfast, lunch, and dinner. Obviously, that takes a toll and gets you on cholesterol medications . . . and potentially stents in your left anterior descending artery. (Not that I know anything about that.)

When you neglect your nutrition, it impacts your energy level because, again, your body needs to break down what you're consuming. When you eat foods that aren't really beneficial, your body is fighting that and trying to figure out Where I sort this? It's kind of like throwing your garbage and recycling down the chute. If somebody has to sort it, they have to go through and say, " Okay, this is recyclable. This is compost. This is actually garbage." Your body has to do that with everything you consume.

It's not just food that has to be sorted—it's information, too. So if you are constantly watching the news or reading posts on all the doom and gloom of the world, guess what? That's going to impact your approach to life. If you focus on negative things, you're inviting them to be a normal part of your life. What you consume makes you. Now, I'm not saying to ignore what's going on in the world, but I am saying take it in and let it pass through you. Adopt the mindset that this is happening in the world, but not happening directly to you.

When there's doom and gloom in the world, ask yourself if you can do something about it. If you can't, then don't worry about it. Is it impacting you directly? No? Don't worry about it. Don't focus your time and energy on things you cannot control. Focus your time and energy on doing what you can do to make your world better. Change comes within, and if you want to change the world, change yourself. If you change yourself and you become a better person, then your impact on the world is going to be better. (And that's something you need to repeat every day. Wash, rinse, and repeat.)

If you're burned out, you're neglecting yourself with what you're consuming. You're also neglecting yourself by avoiding the things that bring you joy and fulfillment. Neglecting yourself will increase your likelihood of either burning out or be staying in a burned-out state for much longer than you want to. It's crucial for you to take care of yourself. You have to be the best version of yourself in order to impact others.

After you stop neglecting yourself and focus on your self-care, you worry about what other people think because you're taking care of yourself. They're going to project onto you what they think : "You're being selfish," " You don't care anymore," or whatever. That's them projecting their beliefs, their thoughts, and their feelings onto you. Be like Captain America : use your shield and block that.

Make sure that you're focusing on yourself first. If you are your best self, what's going to happen when you serve others ? You're going to give them a version that they have never seen before, and it's going to be better than they've ever seen before. You're going to have a huge ripple effect on them and everything else you do.

Don't neglect yourself: when you do, it's going to create some long-term problems. I highly recommend the Disease To Please book. I read it last Christmas, and I 've marked it on my calendar to read it again every Christmas. It's a gift to myself: it allows me to look at what I am doing and see if I am trying to please people instead of serve people. It's a big difference.

OFFSIDE

Next up in the BURNOUT acronym is the letter O, for offside. I'm a huge sports fan, but I wasn't very good at playing. I played basketball and baseball as a kid, but my asthma and body size as a youth created a barrier to pursuing a career in sports. It was a self-imposed barrier, looking back. I could have made changes.

I could have taken better care of myself as a child. I could have chosen to be a little bit more athletic and to practice.

You can improve yourself and you can actually stay in the game and be in balance. When you're burned out in the game of life, you're offside. You're out of bounds. Your body is using all its energy to repair the damage that burnout causes. When you're off sides or out of bounds, you're not in the game. When you're not in the game of life, you're not doing the things that you want to do because you're too damn tired to do it. And why are you so tired? Because your body is using all of its energy to fight the damage that you're doing to yourself.

BURNOUT IS A CHOICE.

Okay, I know that may not be a popular statement, butI'll say it again: you chose to be burned out. The path you chose created the situation. You say, " Well, I'm working too many hours. My boss is a jerk." Blah, blah, blah, blah, blah. It's all true. I don't know your boss, but I'm guessing he or she is a jerk. Don't forget you chose to work there, though. You continue to work there at the time you're reading this book (so to speak). Jobs are still plentiful. Now, that may change. We do have economic ups and downs. But in this world of opportunities, there are things you can do. Yes, I know there are other factors. You may have a mortgage payment that requires you to earn a certain level of income. Again, a choice; no one signed that lease agreement or that mortgage document for you. You did.

You chose that. You choose where you live. You choose what you eat. You chose your partner. You chose your job. You chose the car you drive. You chose the clothes you wear. You chose to subscribe to Netflix. Instead of going to a gym, you are choosing these things. You can do what you want, but your choices do have an impact on your life. What you choose today impacts your life down the road. If you're burned out, it's a choice. You chose to be out of bounds with your life. But here's the crucial thing: you can also choose to get back into the game. My hope for you is that you are making that choice.

UPHEAVAL

Burnout can turn your life completely upside down. When I had my burnout in 2009, you can say that an upheaval took place in my life. For those of you who are not familiar with my story, over a period of 369 days (which I will discuss further in Chapter 4), I had a heart attack that should have killed me. I lost my job during an economic recession. The family vehicle was repossessed. And then, finally, our home was foreclosed. All in a year. I don't want anybody to go through that. It was not fun for my family or me to experience those losses. But we did—and as I said in an earlier post, burnout is a choice. I chose that path.

The decisions I made led up to those 369 days of worst-case scenarios. No one wants to lose his or her health. No one wants to lose his or her job. Having your family car towed away is not a pleasant sight. And going up to your house and seeing a huge padlock and a foreclosure sign on the door is not pleasant, either. It wasn't fun, but I'll tell you what—I'm thankful for all of those things because they woke me up.

Many people are asleep at the wheel when they make the choices that lead to their burnout. They think, Okay, this is where I am, and they don't give themselves permission to change it. You chose burnout, and you can choose a different path in your life. You can do what you want, but you should choose not to be burned out.

Now, I'm not about to tell you to change your beliefs or your faith or anything like that. That's not what this is about. Your life is in upheaval, and you made choices that created this situation.

Would you say, "You know what I want to do? Next year, I think I'm going to burn out "?

Nobody does that. But the choices you make can still lead to burnout, nonetheless. So you have to make better choices to get out of burnout. I talked to a lot of people and they say, " Oh,

I've had burnout a couple times." And my first reaction to that is that once is enough ! Why go through burnout twice? They obviously applied a Band-Aid to their deep, infected wound, but it was still there festering. When it flared up again, they dealt with it again. And my hunch is that, unless they did some deep work to figure out why they burned out in the first place, it's gonna come back. (Sorry for the spoiler!)

My goal when I work with organizations is to identify the root causes of their team's burnout so we can address those issues. When you address the root cause, you prevent it from happening again. Burnout once in your life is definitely enough. I don't want another 369 days ever again. I don't want anybody to go through that, either. And it's preventable. But the key is that you have to choose to prevent it. Is your life in upheaval? Are you offside? Or are you in balance? Are you living the life you choose to live?

TIME

Many people say they don't have enough time. Last time I checked, everyone gets the same amount of time every day. It's how we choose to spend our time that makes the difference. Too often, we say we don't "have time" to do this or this or that. We don't have time to make our own food, so we order fast food. We don't have time to exercise, although we'll spend six hours on our phones or five hours watching Netflix. I'm not asking you to work out for five hours ; just carve out fifteen, twenty minutes. If you're not going to the gym at all, literally carve out five minutes. Go to the gym. Go in there for five minutes and then leave. I guarantee you will feel weird leaving after five minutes. You're going to ask yourself, Why am I leaving? I might as well stay a little bit longer.

I'm a big fan of matching your workload to your energy. I have resources on how to track your energy and your workload so they can match up better. I tend to be a morning person, so I tend to schedule my mornings with tasks and schedule my afternoons with follow-ups. Sometimes it bleeds over, and I have to do main tasks in the afternoon or follow-ups in the morning. If you can somehow structure your days to be a little bit more consistent, though, your body will get into a rhythm. And we've already talked about how rhythm will help you use your time better. I think that's what we really want to see here: spending our time the way we want to, so we feel that we're in a little bit more control than we were before.

CHAPTER 2
HOW DO WE CATCH BURNOUT?

A decade ago, I was the poster child for burnout. I had all the symptoms:

Fatigue
Restlessness
Insomnia
Anger Management Issues
Irritability
Proneness to Mistakes
Relationship Challenges
Physical Challenges
Bad Eating Habits

That list isn't all- inclusive, but I had all of the above, and then some. Everyone knew I was burned out . . . except me. Maybe subconsciously I knew, but on the surface, this Type-A personality would have nothing to do with burnout.

I was in my third year of running a medical clinic. We had never really gotten past the "start-up" phase, mostly because we hadn't decided what the next phase would look like. Our clinic was supposed to have a new building (which they did get, at least half a decade after my 369 Days kick off.)

I was in full-on *git-'er-done* mode, and I never let up. Not resting or taking a break, my body eventually did break, and it kicked off my year of worst-case scenarios. I was beyond foolish back then, not putting myself first, but focusing on pleasing others before myself. It nearly cost me my life. Never again.

Why did I deny my own burnout? I was all about People pleasing. People pleasers are prideful about their accomplishments, and they've likely risen through the ranks of employment and are viewed as an all-star employee. They enjoy that designation, and they don't want to let anyone down, nor lose the view people have of them.

Another component of burnout is Adrenaline addiction. When you're accomplishing a lot, you get excited and invigorated by (and addicted to) the emotions you feel. However you don't take time to smell the roses.

Ignoring the signs. Burnout does not happen overnight. It's not like you wake up tomorrow and say " Oh crap, I'm burned out today." Burnout creeps up slowly over time . . . but when it hits, you'll hit the mat faster than if you were on the receiving end of a Mike Tyson hook.

Ignoring your build up to burnout will cost you.

CHAPTER 3
WHAT DOES BURNOUT LOOK LIKE?

When you are in a state of burnout, your motivation is nowhere to be found. Often, you wish you could just sit and do nothing (which is ironic, because a great way to prevent burnout in the first place is to rediscover boredom). Your energy is depleted, and any energy your body has is channeled towards repairing the damage that stress and burnout have caused. Your emotional well- being is damaged as a result, and you end up being extra moody, possibly showing signs of depression.

HOW YOU VIEW EVERYTHING WILL DETERMINE HOW EVERYTHING HAPPENS IN YOUR LIFE.

When you're stressed, your ability to make clear decisions is reduced. Your brain is allocating power to deal with the aftermath of stress. Think about it: When you're tired, and someone asks you what you would like to have dinner, it's not an easy decision, is it? That's because your brain isn't fully available to you. It's programmed to allocate resources towards what your body is asking for. If your body is in pain, your brain is trying to fix that pain. If you're tired due to lack of restful sleep, you have aches, so your brain will focus on those aches. See the trend?

Stress takes away your mental and physical energy.

You have a choice to be burned out or not. It's up to you. No pill, person, guru, or spiritual leader can change that. It's on you, boss. (But do seek guidance if you're highly stressed or burned out, because an outside point of view can guide you to the best steps to take)

When I was going through my burnout, I was not a nice person. Everyone knew I was burned out except me. I didn't read the memo. I was short with people, frustrated over little (and big) things, and felt that I was carrying the weight of the world on my shoulders, both at work and at home.

NOT A GOOD SITUATION FOR ANYONE.

While I feel there are many factors that lead to burnout, an HBR article suggests six causes of burnout:

Workload
Perceived Lack of Control
Reward
Community
Fairness
Mismatch of Values

When you are stressed out at work, and your boss dumps more work on you, how does that feel? If you're anything like me, you'll go through all kinds of emotions like anger and frustration. Working long hours leads you to take shortcuts such as eating right, taking breaks away from your workspace, exercising, etc. (A note for employers: a 2017 HBR article indicated that US employers pay close to $190 Billion annually due to lost labor being out on leave. We all have a responsibility to address burnout.) Job burnout is a special type of stress. It's a state of physical, emotional, or mental exhaustion combined with doubts about the competence and the value of one's work.

Here's a list of common reasons for employee burnout:

Working more overtime hours than usual
Working on the weekends
Mood swings
Irritability
Decrease in quality of work
Less socializing and more insolation than usual
Fatigue
Increase in sick days or personal days
Disengagement
Unusual sensitivity

When you feel you no longer have control over a situation, your emotions will flare up, and if this is sustained over a period of time, burnout will rear its ugly head. If your life is missing rewards—things you enjoy in life—burnout is definitely a possibility. If you visit the resources page at BreakfastLeadership. com, you can grab a free bucket list worksheet that will help you add back those rewards in your life.

When you are in a burned-out state, you often isolate yourself from others. This cuts out the community of support we all need in life. We gravitate to communities that feel like a part of us, and we can grow and contribute to these communities.

Fairness is a funny concept. I've had employees stop their feet and say a situation was "not fair." Yes, a grown-ass adult did that. They overreacted(in my opinion) to a minute change in procedures. That person later came back to apologize for their behavior, but I realized that their mini meltdown had other components that they brought to the table. Each of us should know what our core values are. At BreakfastLeadership.com/ resources, you can download a free Core Values worksheet to further identify your core values.

If your core values differ from your workplace, you are inviting high stress and burnout to your solo dance party. Burnout has many flavors (flavours in Canada):

Fatigue
Anger
Apathy
Weight Changes
Relationship Stress
Addiction

Fatigue is a culmination of other emotional and physical issues that can lead to burnout. Lack of sleep, poor diet, not taking enough breaks, and having your mind full of things will bring on fatigue symptoms. Fatigue and prolonged stress can lead to various illnesses, both short-term and long-term.

When you're not getting your way, when you're not feeling well, or when you feel the world is against you, anger may set in. Becoming angry over minuscule things is definitely a warning sign of burnout. Remember to breathe!

Apathy, in my opinion, is one of the key red flags with burnout. When you no longer care or show emotion about things that you used to be passionate about, you should definitely be concerned.

During my burned-out state leading up to my 369 Days, I lost interest in going to baseball games. From 2005 to 2008, I was a mini-season ticket holder for the Detroit Tigers. My love for baseball goes back to 1977, when I bought my first pack of Topps Baseball Cards and learned how to calculate the stats on the back of the cards. (Yes, my geekdom goes back decades.) I listened to baseball on the radio and fell asleep to Ernie Harwell calling all of those "long gone" home run calls.

In 2008, however, I barely went to any of the games. My workload was so heavy that I was too fatigued and apathetic to care. I should've seen this huge warning sign, but I ignored it. Big mistake. During my lead up to burnout, my weight gains were noticeable. I easily put on forty extra pounds between

2004 and 2009, which does wonders for your blood pressure and cholesterol readings (please note my sarcasm). When you're stressed and burned out, the body does damage control instead of maintenance.

My relationships suffered during my burnout as well. Not going to baseball games and not visiting my friends as often definitely prolonged my burned-out existence. Another warning sign I ignored: I was also irritated with my spouse and children. I'm not proud of myself about that, but as my kids say now, "Dad's much happier these days."

When you're stressed or burned out, you often seek external "hits" to take away the pain or dull it. Mine, ironically, was spending time on the computer. Note that smartphones didn't take off until the iPhone was introduced in 2007, but I didn't get my hands on one until late 2011. I can't imagine how much worse my addictions would have been if I had my iBinky back then.

CHAPTER 4
369 DAYS

On May 22, 2019, I celebrated the ten- year anniversary of my heart attack.

Why in the world would someone want to celebrate such a scary event? Because I'm thankful for that cardiac event. I'm thankful that I'm still alive, and that I survived that health scare. Statistics indicate that I shouldn't have survived. So you could say that I should be dead instead of alive. Well, thankfully I'm not dead. Those familiar with my story know what transpired after that heart attack. Seventeen weeks after my heart attack, I lost my job during the economic recession. Six months after the job loss, the bank repossessed our family vehicle One month later, the bank foreclosed our home.

Heart attack, job loss, car repossession, home foreclosure—all in a year. I'd call that a crappy year. If I'd had a dog at the time, I probably would have lost it too. (That's a joke . . . you can laugh!)

I'm thankful that all of those things happened. "What?" you may ask, wondering if you read that right. Yes, I'm thankful that I went through all of those situations. They were lessons that I needed to learn. I was on a highway to death. I didn't have boundaries around my working hours, so I was answering and sending emails at all hours of the day, night, and weekend. I was eating fast food for my meals.I was not exercising at all. My sleep was crap. I no longer enjoyed the things of life that used to be an absolute joy to experience.

I WAS COMPLETELY BURNED OUT.

Sometimes the only way to learn is to go through challenges so you can finally make some adjustments. My hope is that no one ever experiences the year I had a decade ago, but if that's the only way for you to make the necessary tweaks to your life, then so be it.

I have always been one to get back up. A fighting mentality is part of my background. Not a confrontational kind of fighting, but fighting to get back on your feet. Fighting to get back in the ring and do the things that you need to do. After all, we all have a calling to do something to make a dent in the universe. I have that calling, and it's with boundaries. It's teaching people how to find their boundaries so that they can have the life they're supposed to have, not be in constant stress about trying to accomplish everything but actually accomplishing nothing.

After all of those events, I was at square one. I had to start from scratch—clean slate, tabula rasa—which for some would be devastating. For me, it was a wonderful opportunity to say, "Okay, let's go ahead and rebuild my life." (Which I did.)

You don't rebuild a forty-something-year-old life in a couple weeks. It takes time. It's taken me several years after those 369 days to determine what is important in my life and what isn't. I had to ask myself, "What are the things that I want to do with my career, and what are the things that I don't want to do with my career?" Once you figure these things out, your life will go a lot easier. When you start from square one, you can redesign your life based on the skills you built in the life that you've lived before.

Now, a decade later, I talk about boundaries and burnout. I see way too many people stressed to the max, burned out, working too many hours, spending hours and days on their iBinkies, and completely missing out on what really matters. You have a choice: boundaries in your life, or a burned-out life. Choose wisely.

You can pick and choose the things that work, and I was able to do that. I went back to the same job—different company, but the same job that I was in when I had my cardiac event. I'm in the same field. Most people would say, "You're crazy to go back in the field that almost killed you." It was important to do this because I knew I had a lot to accomplish, and my career would thrive if I designed my days the way that I needed to (and if you do this, your career will thrive as well).

I am thankful for those 369 days because they changed my life. They saved my life, quite frankly. If I didn't make those changes, I can all but guarantee I wouldn't be writing this book right now.

CHAPTER 5

YOU'RE BURNED OUT. NOW WHAT?

Choice. Burnout is a choice. You chose it.

I highly doubt you intended to burn yourself out, though. That would require some very deeply rooted self-harming thoughts and patterns, and if that's the case, I highly encourage you to seek help immediately.

In the book Disease To Please, Harriet Braiker discusses how many of us have this desire to please others, and oftentimes we put ourselves last, in order to do this. We do too much, too often, for others. We almost never say "no" when someone asks something of us. We suck (like I did) at delegation. We become overwhelmed and we spread our lives too thin.

When we're afflicted with the Disease to Please, we often act to avoid fear, conflict, rejection, and confrontation. Here's the wrinkle: avoiding fears only causes them to intensify. Avoiding conflict creates more internal conflict. Trying constantly to please others basically turns a deaf ear to your inner voice, so you ignore your own personal needs and desires. This causes internal stress, anxiety, depression, and other health challenges, which ultimately leads to—you guessed it—burnout.

How do you fix these things?

Kill the "Shoulds"

"I SHOULD HELP THAT PERSON GOING THROUGH A PERSONAL TRAGEDY."

"I should spend twenty minutes listening to that person complain about her work life (when they won't actually do anything about it because they're doing their own avoidance exercise)."

In both of these examples, you are taking on the burden of others. Noble? Yes. Stupid? Definitely. Be a sympathetic listener, give suggestions, but stop lifting their baggage.

ADJUST YOUR THINKING CHAIR

Steve from the kids' show Blue's Clues had a thinking chair that he sat in when he was solving mysteries with his dog Blue. Thinking can be useful, but your thinking can also lead you to burnout if your thought patterns go to the worst-case scenario by default. To quote the classic Bob Newhart skit, *"Stop it!"*

Your thinking patterns need to be rational, reasoned, and accurate as possible . . . but please, please, please reduce the emotions and feelings you attach to your thoughts. Blame your amygdala! These thinking patterns can easily lead to depression as well.

PEOPLE SHOULD TREAT ME THIS WAY

As Braiker writes in Disease To Please, " *Holding on to conditional beliefs about how people should behave toward you because of all you do for them will only set you up to feel disappointment, anger, and resentment to people in particular as well as disillusionment about others in general.*"

In my book *Pre-Emptive Strike Leadership*, which I co-authored with Dr. Arlene Battishill, we discuss the concept of stand-ins, or people that remind us of someone else. Your boss could remind you of your Dad, who wasn't there for you, or didn't give you the love you expected. Or your co-worker could be a stand-in for someone you worked with years ago who "stole" your girlfriend.

If you're burned out, it didn't happen overnight. There isn't a magic pill that will immediately cure you. It took time for burnout to appear, and it will take time to undo what created your burnout in the first place.

ROUTINE

I am a person of routine. My keys are always in the same spot as my wallet. My outfits are standardized—I don't have to think about what kind of shirt or undergarments I'm going to wear, because they're all the same. Is that "boring ?" Sure, but you know what? For me, consistency plays a huge key in allowing me to think about the things that I truly should be thinking about, and not asking myself, Okay, what shirt should I wear today? What socks go with this tie? If you're consistent in your wardrobe, you save hours of your life every year.

Get clothes that fit. If you've got clothes that you plan to wear when you drop those twenty pounds, here's my recommendation: donate them. They 're not motivating you to lose weight. I hate to be harsh, but it didn't motivate me, so I donated those clothes, and now I'm on a path to losing weight. (But guess what? Now I' ll have to buy new clothes. Well, it'll help the economy.)

Routines are important because when you follow routines, it's going to make life a lot easier.

Here's another example, as silly as it is. We don't have a water dispenser in our fridge, but I have this huge water filter pitcher that I make sure is full every night. First thing in the morning, before I go to the gym, I will fill up my water bottle, and I'll have cold, filtered water to work out with. If I didn't fill the pitcher the night before, then in the morning I have to grab the pitcher, fill it up with water, and pour myself a bottle of lukewarm water. Nothing tastes better than lukewarm water . . . said no one ever. By taking a minute or two the night before to set everything up for the next day, I start off each day smoothly, without resistance or friction.

You have enough resistance in your life. As soon as you get to work, I guarantee you're going to find some resistance—whether it's with a vendor, employees, management, the environment, traffic, or air temperature. (There's no office on the planet that is at the right temperature. It's either too hot or too cold. It doesn't matter who you are.) You're going to be fighting all day with these little nuances. Why should you fight the nuance of not having your water bottle ready, or your clothes picked out? Habits are hard to implement, but as Eben Pagan says, "You have to install a habit." Just like you install an app onto your phone, you have to install a habit. You have to do things the right way in order for it to be successful. If you say, "All right, I'm going to exercise every day," your chance of success is minimal unless you install mechanisms in your day to make it next to impossible to not do.

You literally have to install a habit into your life. Once you do, you're going to see improvements in other facets of your life. I'm doing that right now, and at the time of writing, I'm on a different eating routine and I've lost almost thirty pounds. Believe me, I notice it. I notice how I feel better. I notice my energy levels. I think once I get to the weight that I'm going to get to—and I'm going to get to it because I've installed this eating routine as a habit—I will definitely share with you what I've done, how I've done it, and who I've worked with. I'm absolutely amazed at the results so far.

Here's something that also Eben likes to talk about a lot, and I want you to write this down, please: "Whatever you resist, persists." If you're resisting a change in your life, it will persist, so you need to stop resisting it. Whenever you face a challenge or you feel stressed in your life, feel it. Don't fight it, feel it. Sammy Hagar has a song about that. (Buy Sammy's stuff. I love the guy.)

Implementing boundaries at work, while easier said than done, is crucial. If you have strong boundaries at work, it will make your boundaries at home a whole lot easier to roll out. When you get home, you shouldn't be doing work. Now, for entrepreneurs and people that have really complex jobs, I get it. I've been there. I've worked in IT before—you're basically on call like a physician. If you're a senior leader, you're also on call, although how strong your team is, how well you delegate, and how firm your boundaries are can minimize the impact your work life will have on your home life.

Focusing on boundaries at home is equally important. I'm a big fan of routines. They don't make life boring. I know some people feel that they do, but in my opinion, routines make your life easier! They can automate a lot of things in your life, which frees you up to do the things you really enjoy. You can go to that last minute concert or that last minute sporting event. You can go to dinner somewhere and not have to worry about work.

Set up your home life in a way that works for you and the people you live with. If you're married or have a partner, communicate with them just like you'd communicate with your boss. Let them know what's going on. If you have to do work— for example, if there's a special project that you need to spend time on after hours or at home—let them know. Give them an estimate of how long it will be, and it makes things easier. But again, having control of how you spend your time goes a long way. If you're just going through life aimlessly, not really designing how you spend your time, then your time will get away from you. Then, you won't be able to do the things you really want to do when the opportunities come up.

In the mornings, I work out, brush my teeth, shower—you know, all the fun stuff that you're supposed to do to be nice to the human race. Then I go to work—and when I'm at work, I do my work. When I get home, there's chores (emptying the dishwasher, doing the laundry, all the tedious, boring stuff). If you don't have a ton of clothes, then what happens is you have to use laundry a little bit more frequently. Now work with me here. I know laundry seems like something you already have to do all the time. Yes, but having fewer clothes forces you to be consistent when you do the laundry . . . because if you aren't, you're going to be out of [insert undergarment name here]. That's never a good thing.

Structure your home life in a way that works for you. I'm the first to admit, it takes time ! You're not going to roll it out and say "Okay, here's my life. It's designed perfectly." Things happen, things come up. I'm a big fan of having slack in my life. Let's say I don't do the laundry on a Thursday night like I typically do. "All right," I say to myself, " then I'll do it Friday night or early Saturday morning; we'll figure it out." (And hopefully I don't run out of underwear!) You need some slack in your life to do anything. I know that might seem confusing. I just said to design your life and structure it in a certain way. Then, all of a sudden, I'm telling you cut yourself slack? But here's the trick: structuring and simplifying your life will actually give you the freedom to go easy on yourself.

Chapter 6

RECOVER FROM BURNOUT: THE BUCKET LIST

Batman is my favorite superhero—in fact, he's my favorite character, period. I've been a fan since I was a little boy. (Batman turned eighty in 2019, and recently I entered my fifties, so I've been a fan of his for quite some time!) In life, we each have things that bring us joy and happiness. For me, reading or watching something about the Dark Knight does just that. What brings you joy and happiness? Here is an exercise for you: grab a few sheets of paper and draw a vertical line down the middle of the sheets of paper (That's hot dog style, or shower style, or whatever you learned in kindergarten). You can also visit BreakfastLeadership.com/Resources and click on "Bucket List."

Next, on the left side of the paper, write down everything (experiences, things, foods, etc.) that you really enjoy. Be as complete as you can be. If you need to take a couple days to finish the list, please do so. After you have completed your list, write down the last time you experienced each item on this list. Write the exact date, if you can remember it.

My hunch is that there are many items on the list that you have n't enjoyed in quite some time. Why aren't you doing things you enjoy? "I'm too busy" or "I don't have time" are B.S. answers. We all get twenty-four hours each day. How we utilize those hours is up to each of us.

The final step is to choose three things from your list and schedule times to do or experience these things within the next ten days. Do not skip these appointments with yourself. Treat them like a crucial meeting with your boss. Get in the habit of taking time for the things you enjoy!

There is one item on my bucket list that I will never get to check off. In the summer of 1990, I had an opportunity to see Eric Clapton and Stevie Ray Vaughan at Pine Knob Theater in Clarkston, Michigan. In the late 80s and 90s, I was fortunate to attend a ton of concerts (before tickets were north of $100), and I'm thankful for each show I attended back in my youth. For some reason, I decided to pass on going to the Clapton/SRV show (likely because it was on a weekday and I preferred going to weekend shows). A short time later, on August 27, 1990, Stevie Ray Vaughan was killed in a helicopter accident. I saw Clapton play a few years later, but unfortunately, I will never get to see SRV play live. I have few regrets in life, but not seeing SRV is one of them, and it's something I cannot fix.

What's on your bucket list that you can still accomplish? I'd love to see your bucket list! Email it to bucket@ BreakfastLeadership.com.

Chapter 7
Sleep & Health

I want to talk to you about high energy and how to get it. I'm not talking about guzzling Red Bull or X-Hour Energy or eighteen thousand cups of coffee, but if that's your thing, go for it. I'm not here to judge.

The key to high energy (Eben Pagan talks about this) is deep renewal. It's an exercise where you deeply renew who you are and what you do. Eben talks about a deep renewal from a physical level: exercise, taking care of yourself, eating really well, finding out the foods that treat you well and eliminating the foods that don't. (Yes, I know that your favorite food probably tastes really, really good, but for many of us, the aftermath of it is not really, really good. It's called extra weight, and that's not good for you or anybody involved.)

It's good to be emotional about some things and really keep in tune with how you handle your emotions. One of the things that Eben talks about is how many of us try to move against the grain of our emotions. If something happens to us and we have an emotional response, we need to ride the wave, really just go with the emotion, feel it. Often, stress and burnout happen because we resist what's happening to us. Feel it, name it, and then move on from it. It makes a big difference.

The third thing that Even mentions is rest. I'm a huge fan of rest—huge. I aim to get at least eight hours of sleep a night. No, I am not a baby (I'm like a baby, though—I've been perpetually twelve for decades), but I find it really crucial to get a proper amount of sleep. I go to bed early, a lot earlier than many people. I'm usually in bed between eight and nine and out by nine thirty.

I'll have the baseball game playing in the background, and I'll fall asleep to it. I've been doing that since I was a kid. I used to listen to Ernie Harwell call Detroit Tigers games. (I loved to hear Ernie talk about baseball.) Then, I'd wake up in the morning to J.P. McCarthy on WJR. I'm used to doing that, and it helps me sleep.

Sleep and rest are crucial. If you can build in naps in your day, by all means, do it! Hopefully your employer allows nap breaks, but you can even take a little nap in your car or go somewhere to rejuvenate. You don't need to take a two-hour nap; twenty minutes can make a big difference.

Next up is breathing. It's amazing how often we do not breathe properly. I'm asthmatic, so for me, breathing is a little bit more challenging. Every breath I take—try to get the Police song out of your head—is crucial. It's crucial for you too, of course. For me, it's a little bit more difficult some days. So, I have to keep tabs on that, and breathing properly helps me do that.

Hopefully, that list will help you figure out how to get high energy . . . and natural energy, without all the additives and stimulants you may be using to keep your energy up. When you do those things, believe me, it will make a big impact in your life.

Lack of sleep leads to burnout, but also has other potentially dangerous side effects, according to an article on WebMD called "Sleep Deprivation Can Lead to Serious Issues." According to the article, sleep disorders and chronic sleep loss can put you at risk for:

Heart disease
Heart attack
Heart failure
Irregular heartbeat
High blood pressure
Stroke

Diabetes
Reduced sex drive
Prematurely aged skin
Automobile accidents
Depression
Memory loss
Weight issues
Judgment

Many people suffer from insomnia every year. Sleep seems like an impossibility for some, and it has a long-lasting impact on your life. According to Mayo Clinic, insomnia symptoms may include:

Difficulty falling asleep at night
Waking up during the night
Waking up too early
Not feeling well-rested after a night's sleep
Daytime tiredness or sleepiness
Irritability, depression or anxiety
Difficulty paying attention, focusing on tasks or remembering
Increased errors or accidents
Ongoing worries about sleep (So ironic. Worrying about sleep can cause you to not sleep)

The symptoms above mimic burnout. When you are burned out, your brain is so focused on addressing the damage from the stress and burnout that your body doesn't have the energy to rest. Let me repeat that.

UNDER STRESS AND BURNOUT, YOUR BODY DOESN'T HAVE ENOUGH ENERGY TO REST.

One of the symptoms mentioned above (waking up during the night) is a huge roadblock to restful sleep. An article from Practical Pain Management discusses potential causes of disturbed sleep, and introduces CBT as a possible option for treatment. Burnout is caused by many factors, but a lack of restful sleep is a huge contributor. If you can't rest, everything else will tumble like a house of playing cards.

There is no shortage of posts on social media saying that sleep is important to reducing stress and preventing (or reducing) burnout. Signs of burnout include exhaustion, insomnia, interrupted sleep, and getting sick more often. If you're burned out, the challenge of getting a good night of sleep is a big one. During burnout, your mind is constantly thinking about work, life, family, responsibilities, and struggles (health, financial, personal) . . . and you often lack the motivation to do anything about it. Sleeping eight-plus hours per night is beneficial, but if your sleep isn't truly restful, then your body will not recover from the toxicity that you take in every day. No wonder you're irritable!

Burnout is real. I had a severe burnout in 2009 that nearly took my life. After a year of significant losses, I rebuilt my life from the bottom-up and learned the importance of restful sleep, and now I live a life with reduced stress and zero burnout. There's hope for all who are going through high stress and burnout, but simply prescribing " Get more sleep!" is just prescribing a band-aid, and it doesn't address the root cause(s) of your burnout.

There are reasons why you are not resting when you sleep. The key is to determine what those reasons are so you can deal with them head- on. For the next week, keep a notepad by your nightstand (not the notes app on your smartphone, but a piece of paper and a writing instrument), and when your mind starts racing about things, write them down. In the morning, review the list, and next to each item, write down why these things are bothering you.

Over the course of a week or so, you should start seeing some trends, and it can help shed light on what is causing you stress and leading to your burnout state. Once you have compiled the lists and can see patterns of what's going on, you need to figure out how to resolve those issues. Easier said than done, but it can be done!

Meditation, yoga, breathing exercises, moments of zen: all important to help you focus on the moment and focus less on thoughts that create anxiety or depression. The challenge, though, is that these are often temporary fixes that don't resolve the root issues. If you are anxious about something that could happen in the future, or if you're depressed about situations that haven't turned out the way you hoped, meditation can help you focus on this moment and put those issues on the back burner. You'll get relief after meditation exercises, and being mindful is a huge help to bring you into the present. But does it fix the problems in your life? Let's look deeper.

We'll start with anxiety. Anxiety is worrying about a possible future state or situation. For example, maybe you're anxious for the results from your medical tests, or you're worried about how your loved one will react to your last- minute work meeting tonight. Meditation and mindfulness can get you focused on this moment, but you need to change the mindset that's causing the anxiety in the first place. You need to create mental boundaries to prevent negative or worrisome ideas from renting space in your head. This takes serious effort to create these boundaries, especially if you've never dealt with boundaries before.

Depression is worrying or being upset about events in the past, or things that led up to feelings today. As with anxiety, you need boundaries to control your thoughts and your reactions.

Having stronger mental and emotional boundaries in your life will make meditation work even better for you, and create a life of less stress, burnout, and other health issues.

CHAPTER 8
WORK AND HOME AND FINANCES, OH MY!

When we are in a role such as a "day job" (as we like to refer to them) or launching a business as an entrepreneur, you have to carefully balance your time. If you don't, your nights and weekends will get gobbled up by work (especially if you work in an entrepreneurial organization).

Your day job requires you to be focused and do the things you're being paid to do. It's not always easy to focus on your day job and your own business, but there are many of us who do it, and we do find it fulfilling. For some of us, we even find that there are synergies between our nine-to-fives and our entrepreneurial endeavors.

The key to drawing boundaries, especially when you're an entrepreneur, is picking the right "one thing" to focus on. There's no shortage of things that you can focus on when you're an entrepreneur : marketing online, podcasts, blog posts, Funnels, and all the things you hear about and read about. It seems like they're all important, that they're all good tools to use.

What you need to do is hone in on what you're trying to accomplish with your organization. What's the core value of what you're offering to your clients? Do that. Go where your clients are. Focus and serve them in that arena. If that's using blog posts and podcasts and Funnels, great. If it's face-to-face conversations, then do that.

There are only so many hours in a day. We've heard that a million times. The key is to spend the right time on the right things: because when you're spending time on doing a hundred things, you'll never get that one thing done. You're going to get, quite frankly, nothing done.

Focus on the thing that you need to get done and get it done. Then celebrate it. It's important to celebrate what you've accomplished because if you just do, do, do without stopping, you're not going to have anything to show for it once you get to that endpoint, whatever that endpoint looks like. Stress happens when you don't have the right boundaries in your life—and specifically, when you're trying to do too much, trying to appease everyone, and you're not taking care of yourself.

It's natural. You feel overwhelmed, which is a stressful situation, which, in turn, creates all types of mental and physical problems. In 369 days, I lost everything. One of the key causes of this was the stress that I was under. I was trying to deliver everything that I was supposed to deliver, whether it was fulfilling unrealistic requests or overextending myself beyond reasonable boundaries or schedules, or the demands of providing for a family, and raising children, and navigating all kinds of different things. It added up, and it created a pretty, pretty chaotic year for me.

You're probably feeling some stress right now. Especially if it's wintertime—winter months tend to be harder than others. We're still kind of reeling, if you're in a winter climate, dealing with the cold weather and the snow. You're possibly still recovering from the holidays.

Whatever the weather, stress is taking a toll on your life and you need to figure out how to address it. I share on Twitter and my other social media platforms a ton of resources on how to manage stress. There are different ways to go about it, but the key elements to take away from are getting proper rest, eating properly, controlling how you spend your time, and getting rid of clutter in your home.

If possible, I highly recommend that you tackle your clutter, because it causes you stress when you're always trying to figure out where things are. If you don't know where your keys are, then every morning, you're stressing out, trying to find them. Find a place for them, put them there. Always. That way, you never lose them. You don't have to think about it. They're just going to be there. Same thing with your clothes: pick your clothes out the night before like your mom told you to. She had the right idea. She was probably just trying to save some time to get you out the door so you didn't miss the bus or you weren't late to school, but choosing your outfit the night before is still a good idea.

In my situation, simplifying my clothes made a big difference. I don't have to think about what I'm wearing. The clothes I have fit (more or less) and everything else that I do on a daily basis is consistent, too. I don't have to think about it. It's on autopilot, just like brushing your teeth, taking a shower, getting cleaned up, all of these things. I don't stress about those routines because I know what's going to happen. I know when I'm going to be doing them, and I do them.

Recently I was late to work because of a snowstorm, and I was a few minutes late for an interview for a position I was hiring for. I was able to message the individual (I was a rider, not a driver, in the car—don't text and drive, people), and tell them that I was going to be a few minutes late, which is not something that typically happens to me. (Quite frankly, I don't remember the last time I was late to something.) But sometimes, things happen, just like snowstorms.

I didn't stress about it. I had the capability to message that person and let them know that I was running late. That immediately relieved my stress. I do not like being late. I feel that it is insulting to the other party when you are not on time. For me, it shows a lack of respect. I'm not harping you if you are somebody that struggles with being on time, but it's something you want to take in mind. It does cause stress to you and to others when you are late, so do your best to be on time.

Most of our waking hours are spent consecutively at our jobs. When you're spending that much time in one place, you might encounter burnout if you don't design your days the right way. Many of us have been at our jobs for a while, so the prospect of changing how we do things without getting approval from our bosses can be traumatic to some, and downright frightening to others. The best way to approach this is to figure out exactly what you want to do, and what your day should look like.

Now, for some of us, we may not know. I can definitely help you get clear on that. Right now, I want to focus on how to approach your boss about changing how you do things. The first step is just to realize that you are approaching burnout . . . or maybe, in a worst- case scenario, you are burned out at work already. Acknowledging that is a huge step. Most people don't even get to that stage. If you're understanding that things aren't right, and that you feel overwhelmed, that's good. It's not good that you're overwhelmed, but it's good that you understand it.

Otherwise, you might go through the motions, and hate your job, and want to leave . . . when, in fact, it may not be the job that's the problem. The issue may be on how you approach your job. Identifying what's bugging you is a big thing. Write down all of the things that bother you about your job. Be open. This is a conversation with yourself, and it doesn't have to be something that you do overnight. You can write it down over the course of a week, maybe even a month.

Depending on the type of work you do, your job may have cycles and seasons. You may want to take a look at those as well and see if there are busier seasons and others that drag you down.

The second thing you need to understand is that how you approach your boss about this is crucial. Hopefully, you have a good communication system with your boss or bosses. If not, then the next step is figuring out how to communicate. The best way to find out is to ask them. Whenever I get a new boss, I always ask, "How would you like me to communicate with you? Do you want it in face-to-face meetings, over emails, a scheduled meeting, free form?" Figure out what their style is and deliver to them the communication in a format that's good for them and for you. If it doesn't align with how you want to communicate, then bring that up.

Once you get the communication all sorted out, the next thing is to approach your boss with your concerns. You may have to do this by being humble. You don't go in as a victim. Don't blame your organization. Definitely don't blame your boss, but approach them and say that you're worried about yourself and that you need some help and guidance. When I'm the boss and people come to me and ask for help, it feels good because, number one, they trust my ability to guide them. Number two, they understand that they need some help to grow. That is a huge step for an individual to be able to do that. Once you do that, then you can sit down with your boss and talk about the different things that are bugging you.

Your boss may not be able to address everything, but at least if they can lift some of the burdens causing you to get burned out, that is a huge win for you. That's a huge win for the organization, too, because it increases the likelihood that you're actually going to stay to stay there instead of burning out and quitting.

CHAPTER 9
THE GREAT PURGE

LIVE SIMPLY, KEEP THE THINGS THAT SERVE YOUR
NEEDS, AND DONATE THE REST.

For the longest time, I dreamed of being a minimalist : someone who would only have a few things and discarded the rest. Walking into a living room that had a couch, a table, a TV, and not much else seemed to be perfect.

The environment I was in was not conducive to my desire for minimalism.

Minimalists often are described as people who have one set of dishes, very few clothes, just the basics. In the smaller condo landscape of Toronto, this style of living is in alignment with the affordability of housing in this ever-growing city.

A few years ago I read Essentialism by Greg McKeown, which altered my perspective on things, and experiences. Where minimalism is to have limited items, essentialism is to have the items that are essential to your desired life.

I used to have a huge DVD and CD collection, plus a bunch of comic books, baseball and hockey cards, memorabilia, and so on. Most of those items have been sold and/or donated. I stream my music, and when I do watch movies or TV, I use streaming services or OTA (no cable!). My books are mostly of the ebook flavor (although I tend to receive a couple dozen books every year to read and review. Great gig!). Now my life consists of things that are essential to accomplishing what I want to do in life.

I don't need to rent a storage locker. I don't have a basement full of things that I haven't touched in months or years. People fail to realize they are spending money to store things they don't use. Many people are paying utilities on larger properties to have rooms that serve no function but to store things that may have been of use in the past, but no longer are.

Much like the exercise of purging activities from your life every six months, you should periodically go through your belongings and see what you're no longer using. Someone else could use those things, so donate them. When you have the things that are essential, you can help reduce your burnout, because you're not suffering with the clutter (or financial burden) of storing all of those things.

THE TO- DO LIST

Make yourself a good cup of coffee or tea, and let's grab your to-do list. You might be at work or you might be at home, but right now, we're going to focus on a work to-do list (but it's applicable to home life, as well).

Go through the exercise and make sure that your to-do list is up-to-date. Make sure that you have all your present commitments listed on this particular sheet (you can also use an electronic to-do system, whatever works). Make sure everything is on there. Do not get overwhelmed—because my hunch is, it's a rather robust list of things. Once you go through this and you look at everything, I want you to look at things that are basically things that could lose you your job if they don't get done. Highlight those (or, if you don't have a highlighter, put a star by them). Hopefully that entire list is not stars. If it is, then we've got a challenge ahead of us ! Ideally, you want to highlight the really crucial things that need to get done.

The next step is to figure out from those starred lists, what are two things—not three, not ten, but two—that you could possibly get done either today or this week. Write those two things on another sheet and label that sheet Most Important Tasks. Write those two things down. Nothing else goes on that sheet. The other to-do sheet that you filled everything out on ? File that away. Grab that sheet with the two tasks. Those are what you are going to work on, and you're going to work on them until those things are done.

Remember, I told you to highlight (or star) the things you 're confident you could complete either today or this week, so don't work on anything else, if at all possible, except those two items on the Most Important Tasks sheet. Once those two tasks are done, cross them off and take that sheet and file it. Don't throw it away, but file it. It might be a good idea to write a date at the top, as well.

Now that you've completed those two tasks, take fifteen minutes—doesn't need to be very long, only fifteen minutes—and don't do anything. If you're working in a factory and there are parts flying by you, I don't recommend this exercise because you'll definitely get the foreman on you really quick. If you're in an office setting, though, take fifteen minutes and just be. Don't do anything. While you're sitting there staring off in space and you have a micromanager who asks you, "What are you doing? How come you're not working ?" then act as if you're doing something. Tidy up the files on your desk, or maybe wipe down your desk if you have cleaning wipes. Get up and stretch. Go use the facilities. Grab a cup of water. Just don't work for fifteen minutes.

You need to celebrate that you have accomplished something. We go from task to task, to task to task, to task to task to task . . . and we don't stop to reflect on what we just did. We forget that we've accomplished something. We've finished something, but we just go into autopilot mode and go round and round and round. No wonder we're burning out. We're not stopping ! Think of the Indy 500 or a NASCAR race. They run around in circles for 500 miles. They finish the race. They're supposed to stop, regroup, and talk about how they did in the race. It's the same with this Most Important Task list. Stop and reflect on what you've accomplished.

Otherwise, what you're doing would be like hitting the 500 mark, winning the race, but then running and running and running until you run out of gas, completely burn out, or wreck.

You need to stop, pause, and say, "Okay. I've done those things. Now I can learn from them." Maybe you did something unique that helped you to create or finish something faster than you had before. Figure that out. You will create a rhythm of work.

Naturally, if you get two things done pretty quickly, you'll be like, "Boom. I can get ten things done today." Don't fall into that trap ! If you finish something early in the day, then look at your list and pick maybe one more thing for the day. Don't try to do more than three a day. If, for some reason, you can get five or six done and get that list cleared out, I'm okay with it, but make sure you take some breaks in between those accomplishments. That way, you will actually feel accomplishment. See how it feels, and then you'll get into the rhythm.

After you do your Most Important Tasks, look at your original list and see if there's anything on that list that somebody else should be doing instead of you? Highlight those as well. Use a different color highlighter or a different symbol (maybe a box or a circle), then talk to your supervisor and say, "I think this person would be better to work on this, and here's the reason why." Also show your boss what you've already accomplished then say, "Look at all the things that I've accomplished, but I think these things here Jill would be able to do better." That could be a slippery slope, because your boss may say, "Well, you're getting everything else done. Why don't you wanna do that?" I have one phrase for you for that : "Resume.doc."

If you have a micromanaging boss like that, that's not the best environment in the world for you to be in. There's other opportunities out there. Go find them.

CHAPTER 10
SUCCESSFUL MORNINGS

Wake up at the same time every day. I know many of us use an alarm clock to wake up on work days, but not on the weekends. Your body is not a big fan of ups and downs, though. It craves stability. Use your alarm and wake up at the same time every day. Once your body gets used to this, you'll thank me.

Would this require you to go to bed at the same time every day? Yes, I recommend doing that to get an ample amount of restful sleep every day. I know that life doesn't always provide for this opportunity. You have guests from out of town, so you'll stay up late. Or you have tickets to that sold- out concert or sporting event. By no means am I suggesting you miss out on those things.

On the contrary, I'd suggest taking time off of work to do them! (Please don't have your boss email me on that one.) Out-of-town guests and concerts aside, I know that I'm a better employee when I'm rested. My ability to focus improves when I've had decent sleep over time.

And don't forget to do things that bring you happiness and pleasure. You're not a robot ! When you are happy and rested, you're a better employee, a better family member, a better lover, a better person for your community.

EXERCISE

There are countless studies on the benefits of exercise. With so many health apps and devices for our phones, there's never been an easier time to track your activity than today. My phone counts my steps, so I do my best to hit ten thousand steps per day. Some days are easier than others, but ironically, I easily surpassed ten thousand steps without even thinking about it. I was attending a week's worth of conferences, and from walking to the train station to walking around the various conference halls and exhibits, I easily surpassed ten thousand steps. Be sure to seek approval from your medical provider to make sure what exercises are right for you.

I suggest investing the money into a personal trainer, even if it's only for an intro session. You'll learn how to properly use the exercise equipment, and you'll also learn the steps to exercising properly. You'll have more energy, your stress levels will drop, and your stress management will improve. My suggestion is to work out first thing in the morning. I know many people don't like waking up early, but by getting up at the same time every day, you can do this as well. Be sure to drink water when you first wake up. That kick starts your body and gets it ready to attack your day.

Exercise is crucial for your life, and oftentimes, people don't realize that exercising is actually putting boundaries in your life. Let me explain. For years, I didn't exercise and I experienced the aftermath of what happens when you don't take care of yourself. Hint: 369 days.

Exercise is one of those things where if you're not used to doing it, you're not going to be able to jump right into it. If you're going to start an exercise program—this is going to sound like a commercial—talk with a medical professional to come up with an idea. Don't just jump into it, because you will hurt yourself if you don't know what you're doing. Start off small, start off slow, and you'll go a long way in making some changes in your life from a physical standpoint.

I spend a lot of time on the treadmill, a little bit on weights. I'll be changing that up a little bit. I need to really work on some tone and really help build some muscle mass for metabolism. For me, exercise is an excellent way to manage stress, especially because I work out in the morning. However, many people may work out at night. They may work out in the afternoon if they have the time and space for it.

Whatever time works for you, do it. Don't wait. Do your best to get your exercise in as frequently as possible. Whether that's just simply walking to lunch instead of driving to lunch, or parking further out in the parking lot and walking, those extra steps make a big difference.

For stress management, though, exercise is great because it gives you those endorphins. At the end of the day, I feel better after working out. Also, when I work out in the morning, it gives me energy to handle stress a little bit better than if I didn't. When you're dealing with issues at work, things that come up or in life, life changes, or whatever, the exercise really makes a big difference.

My homework for you is to start exercising if you're not. If you are exercising, awesome. Take a look at what you're doing and make sure that it's working for you. Hopefully, you will see some positive results once you start.

EAT BETTER

I ate cereal as a kid. A LOT of cereal. The sugary, toy- in- the- bottom- of- the- box kind of cereal. Not exactly the best way to start your day. We ask our bodies to put up with a lot during the day, so shouldn't we provide them with something to help them fight the good fight? Each person has their dietary requirements, so I won't say what you should or shouldn't eat. I'll leave that between you and your nutritional counselor. My diet varies in the morning, other than the staples of water, tea, or coffee (yes, I drink both). I'll eat oatmeal, yogurt with granola and fruit, or the classic bacon 'n' eggs.

SIMPLIFY YOUR ATTIRE.

For an easy entrance into your day, I cannot recommend enough that you pick out your clothes the night before. Did you know your brain consumes calories, just like your body does? Why would you waste the precious morning brain power, by wrestling with what to wear?

If you live in a climate where the weather varies dramatically, then I suggest looking at your weather app the night before, to see what the temperatures will be the next day. In the spring and fall seasons where I live, the mornings can be cold and afternoons warm, so layers are important.

One other pro tip I have for you on attire (which works well for men) is to standardize your clothing. Buy the same socks, undershirts, and underwear. Also have at least two weeks' supply of each, so you're not constantly needing to do laundry (another pro tip!). I have a preferred brand of undergarments and socks, and by having the same type of socks, laundry is a lot easier when matching up pairs of socks. Who wants to spend their life trying to match up socks?

Not this guy.

For slacks and shirts, you should have some variety, but go with the style and color (colour in Canada) that best fits you. Spend the money on quality attire, and it will last you a long while. It will help you when you put on your clothes, your attire will fit you the way you want it to. Be sure to mix up your shirts, though. You don't want people thinking you only have one shirt! (It worked for Steve Jobs and Mark Zuckerberg though, so if you can only have one kind of shirt, go for it, boss.)

JOURNAL

I'm a huge fan of journals. I encourage you to journal your days so you can look for personal growth opportunities and notice trends in how your days and weeks are going. Journaling allows you to get what 's in your head onto paper, so you can review it later and see where you are today compared to when you wrote your note. Journaling your challenges and stressful situations is helpful, as it can provide clues to what's causing the stress in your life and how you can reduce (or hopefully eliminate) those stressful times.

I love to write. Whether it's tweets or longer posts, it's helpful for me to write what I'm thinking or feeling. Writing down what's going on in your life is good for the soul, as you can empty the things you're thinking onto paper (or a digital tool like Evernote) helps you shift those events out of your mind and into something you can see. You don't have to write a novel (unless you want to!). I tend to write about my experiences from the day before, or just things that come to mind. There's no rules here, it's your journal!

I do recommend having one place to write, if you're using technology. Our digital toolboxes can get as cluttered as a junk drawer if we're not methodical in what we do. I like Evernote because I have the app on my phone as well as on my home laptop. The information syncs across all of your devices, so you can pick up where you left off, no matter where you are.

Here's a reflective journaling exercise:

Write what went really well today. Be as detailed as you want. You'll look back at this from time to time, so you'll want to be verbose here.

Write what went "badly" or didn't go as you would have hoped, wanted, or planned. List the experience(s) and write down what your role was in these matters, but don't beat yourself up. Write from a factual standpoint.

Write down what you want to accomplish tomorrow. Be bold. Set big goals, but ones that you feel you can achieve (or at least move forward).

Use your journal daily. Writing things down celebrates what went well, what didn't, and what positive things you'll do tomorrow. It provides you a way to release everything that happened in your day, so that you can get a restful night of sleep, which is a crucial burnout prevention step.

DESIGN YOUR IDEAL DAY

Are you living your ideal day today? I am. I'm writing this chapter on a Saturday, so Saturdays have always been my favorite day. A lot of times, what I find is Saturdays are those days where you don't necessarily have to set your alarm. (Unless you work; then I kind of recommend you do that, unless you can wake up naturally without an alarm. Those people are unique, for sure.) But at the end of the day, you want to make sure that every day is a day that you actually enjoy, and that's why designing your days is so important.

To design the days the way that you want them, it's important to have boundaries in your life. Yes, you have obligations and responsibilities at work and in your personal life. If you're a parent, your children need you to do some things that they can't do. You can line up your days around those responsibilities, but by no means does that mean you have to go and completely give up your life and not enjoy what you want to enjoy. For years, I was constantly going at it. Working long hours on email constantly—working, working, working—of course led to my 369 days of worst-case scenarios.

I've learned from that experience, and it frustrates me to see so many people in that same zone. They're still working, they're still doing all of these things, and they're trying to accomplish so much—but they're not accomplishing anywhere near what they could because there's a lack of focus and a lack of design in their daily lives. We've all gone on autopilot.

Something I find helpful is to literally have a theme for every one of your days. Mondays aren't exactly everyone's favorite, but you should have a theme of what you want to do on a Monday. Same thing for Tuesday through Friday, and your weekends as well. Design them. Have two or three things you know you want to do on a particular day. When you do that, you're gonna get a rhythm of how you do things. You're gonna get to the point where you look forward to weekdays, not just to the weekend. If there's something particular that you like doing on those days, you look forward to a Tuesday or Wednesday.

I want you to focus on what your ideal day and week would look like. Ultimately, what you want to get from this exercise is to get to the end of your day and feel like you had a great day, like you accomplished what you wanted to and then some.

TRIAGE YOUR CALENDAR

How you spend your time is directly tied to how you prevent burnout. It's such an important component to designing your ideal life that it needed its own chapter. See you on the next page!

CHAPTER 11
TRIAGE YOUR CALENDAR

If I had to pick my favorite tip (favourite for my Canadian readers), it would be to triage your calendar. When I began my career, I played an accountant. In that role, I provided services to clients, and I had to track our time, down to fifteen-minute increments (one firm I worked for billed in twelve-minute increments). It's a habit that many would hate, but I keep track of every day with a calendar on my laptop that syncs across my devices. I look at my calendar frequently (maybe too frequently) to see what I've worked on and what's next on my plate.

For a successful day, you should look at the next day the night before. This will mentally prepare you (or scare you) for what you have to face the next day. I also suggest looking at a weekly view of your calendar. That way, you can batch like items together (when possible.)

A deeper subject is when to schedule tasks, meetings, and so forth, through your day. Most of us in management do have some flexibility in our schedules, but even if you are the front lines, you can work with your bosses to establish the best times to meet. My next book on making your schedule match your inner life will go deeper into this subject, with tools on how to discover the best time to perform tasks, hold meetings, and down time, to stay in rhythm with your soul.

I have a favor to ask: over the next month, I want you to keep track of everything you do on your calendar. Now, some of you may already do somewhat this, while others probably don't. Remember earlier when I wrote that I had to keep track of my time in fifteen-minute increments? I did that for well over a decade. It helps you to track billable hours, but it'll also help you be productive, and quite frankly, it's gonna help you establish boundaries. You'll know what you're spending your time on, and you can make the changes that you need to make as a result.

Now, if you're using an electronic calendar, great. It'll be really easy for you to document what you're doing throughout the day. If you use a paper calendar, make sure it's a calendar that you have with you all the time (or at least have a way to document your hours on the go, and use that to update your paper calendar later).

Every day, we have things that we have to do. We have to eat, we have to sleep, and we have to brush our teeth, but there are other things that we do day after day that take time. When you're trying to focus on the things that are important to you, you want to make sure that you're spending the proper amount of time on those things and less time on the routine stuff, if at all possible.

The exercise we've gone through before is looking at your calendar and figuring out how you're spending your time. There's many ways to do this, and reach out to me because I have a system that can help you really get down deep into how you spend your time and you can figure out a way to make life easier for you.

Let's talk about automating and batching tasks that you work on from time to time, every day, or every week. Once you know what those things are, delegate them if you can. If you can't, at least be specific on when you do it and really schedule things. Get comfortable with doing things routinely at the same time every day, or every week, because it'll become part of you, it'll be automatic, you won't have to think about it.

This is one of those things where we like to call a "life hack" that I've discovered over the last few months, and I really wish I had jumped on it before. It's called Amazon Subscribe and Save. This is a life-changing thing. There are so many things that you can order on Amazon and get delivered to your home on a scheduled basis (every month, or every couple of months, depending on what it is). This is going to make you laugh, but I have my toilet paper delivered to me ! Once you pick yourself up off the floor, you' ll realize this is actually a brilliant idea. Why should I spend time going to a store, standing in lines and buying something that I use daily? The cost is actually affordable, especially if you factor in time!

Depending where you live, there are other services you can take advantage of, too. Grocery delivery is an example. It's getting easier and easier to have things brought to you. This actually enables you to spend more time on things that grow you or things that you enjoy. I don't know many people who actually enjoy going to the grocery store. I used to work for a family owned grocery store in my teens, so I'm not allergic to grocery stores or anything, but if there's a way for someone to go shopping for me and bring it to my house, or bring it out to my vehicle, sign me up. By outsourcing things like grocery shopping, you're making time for things that are important to you instead of the boring tasks that you can automate or delegate.

Look at your calendar and look at the things that you're doing. Is there anything there that could be automated, delegated, or just deleted ? When you offload those mundane tasks, you' ll find yourself with more time. When you have more time, you can do things that are important, like relaxing, reflecting, growing—so many possibilities.

CHAPTER 12
YOUR DREAMS AND GOALS

Burnout loves to kill your dreams and goals. You no longer enjoy and look forward to the things that you used to because all of your energy is focused on being burned out. Reconnecting to your values and your goals for your future is a big step to recovering from your burned- out state.

Each year, I review the past year and look forward to the year ahead in terms of goals, bucket list items, and other things I plan to accomplish. Words are important here. I wrote a plan to *accomplish*, instead of *wanting* to accomplish. When it comes to goals, want isn't a strong enough word to use. Want feels like an "It would be nice if . . . " type of word. Planning to accomplish means that I intend to take action and reach my goal, and that sends forth the thoughts to start on the journey.

What do you plan on accomplishing in the next year? The next six months? The next three months? The next month? Next week? Tomorrow? Today? Start planning, and that will plant the seeds for what you plan to accomplish! There are many goal planners and journals out there, but I suggest finding one that is easy for you to use. Paper, electronic, or a mix of both are all fine. Use the tools that are comfortable for you.

I've seen some people establish seven to ten goals per year, with two to three per quarter. That may be a bit much if you're not used to setting goals. I suggest two to three goals for the year, and another two to three goals after that if you're feeling driven. If you accomplish your two to three main goals and tackle a couple more, then you'll have an amazing year! Go to BreakfastLeadership.com/resources and grab the Most Important Tasks sheet to help you establish your goals.

Personal boundaries are important to protect yourself from harm, both harm that others do to you because of their own issues and the harm you do to yourself (especially if you're a people pleaser).

The phrase "It seemed like a good idea at the time" is often associated with regret, pain, and suffering. Just a few of the examples I've heard (or experienced myself) are moving to a more expensive area when your finances are a mess, getting a car loan when buying a used car with cash would be the better choice, or taking that job simply because it paid more, but had a toxic environment.

At work, not having boundaries around your hours of availability is a direct violation of your personal time and space. Would you go into the office at 11 p.m. to work? No, of course you wouldn't. Then why are you answering a work email at 11 p.m.? Most organizations' definition of "emergency" is way off. There are very few legitimate reasons your employer should need to contact you after hours. If the work is truly required after hours, then employers need to hire night staff. There's a reason workplace cultures are suffering. People are tired and burned out because there's a significant lack of boundaries around both the work itself and when it's expected to be performed.

When you lack personal boundaries, you are giving away control of your life. Do you want your boss, lover, or friend to control your life, or do you want to be the pilot of the plane called you? Pausing and reflection on your daily lives helps you summarize the experiences, looking for ways to improve how you conduct your life, as well as minimize any negative self-talk about mistakes and/or things that didn't go as you would have hoped or planned.

Life has a way of providing many triumphs, struggles, victories, losses, ups, and downs. How you think about these experiences dictates how your future will look. Too often we live our lives on auto-pilot, going through the motions, not taking time to smell the flowers (not all of us like roses), take in nature, or simply just be. We jump from activity to activity without pausing, reflecting, and asking, "What just happened to me?"

When was the last time you reflected on an experience you recently had? Some call this a debrief, like you would do in any project management exercise. A debrief requires you to ask tough questions and seek honest answers. What went well? What went sideways? Did we learn anything new? Did any of our past theories help (or hurt) this project? We can use that methodology when we reflect on life experiences as well.

Public speakers can reflect on:

What went well during your talk?
What did you forget to do?
Did you feel the audience was engaged, or were they suffering from after-lunch food coma?

Parents, after having a difficult discussion with their children, can reflect on:

What went well (if anything)?
Did your child seem to understand your point of view?
Did you listen (truly listen) to your child's responses?
Were you in the moment, or were you rehashing the past, or even reliving an experience you had as a child?

Check yourself. Pausing and reflecting on your daily life helps you summarize your experiences, look for ways to improve how you conduct your life, and minimize any negative self-talk about mistakes and disappointments.

The sun still rises, even during winter, and when it's hidden by clouds, it's still there. Whenever you're going through a season of stressful situations, the chances for burnout and stress are high.

You feel like a piñata. Nothing is going right for you. You may feel the world is against you. I know how you feel. I've experienced this in my career, and I know it's not a walk in the park. However, you don't have to let these challenges break you down. You are in control of your mind, your thoughts, your reactions, and how you navigate through this thing we call life.

I want everyone to avoid burnout because it takes away your ability to enjoy life. Nothing feels right or good. You become numb to the things that brought you joy before. That's not fun for anyone—your family, your friends, your co-workers, or you. When you're in one of those seasons where it's You v. The World, there's one key trait that will serve you well.

PATIENCE

Axl Rose sang about it. The Oxford Dictionary defines it as "The capacity to accept or tolerate delay, problems, or suffering without becoming annoyed or anxious." Anxiety, annoyance, and suffering can all lead to stress and burnout, but learning tolerance can reduce your stress and stave off burnout. How do you become more patient? An article in Inc. Magazine gives us some clues:

Wait for things instead of expecting instant gratification.

Stop doing things that are not important to your work and your life.

Be more aware of things that cause you to be impatient. Eliminate those things if at all possible.

Relax and take deep breaths.

Dr. Freudenberger, through his work in burnout, discovered that burnout is robbing our society of high-achievers (both women and men) who society looks up to as leaders and action-takers.

I've seen that many people who are burned out tend to be Type-A personalities: driven, successful, but also not satisfied with their accomplishments,so they keep chasing more and more. This chasing leads to burnout. Burnout often comes with a dulling and deadness feeling within. Things that used to excite us no longer do. We are often numb to the world.

Sound familiar? Am I talking about you right now? If you said yes (either out loud, or whispered to yourself), then you've taken a huge step in admitting you have an issue and that, deep down, you want to fix it.

Now that you have acknowledged you may be burned out, the next key step is to stop the bleeding. You need to pause what you're doing and do a simple breathing exercise for two minutes. Not thirty, not forty-five . . . just two minutes. If you are in a place where you can close your eyes, do so. if not, find a place where you can be safe and without interruption for those two minutes.

Close your eyes. Breathe in for four seconds. Hold your breath for four seconds. Exhale for four seconds. Pause for four seconds. Breathe in for four seconds, hold for four seconds, exhale for four seconds. Pause for four seconds. Repeat this for two minutes (set an alarm or timer on your phone if you need to).

After those two minutes, see how you feel. My hunch is that you'll be a bit more relaxed than before. This is good. This demonstrates that you can unwind a little—and it only takes two minutes.

Implement this breath work throughout your day. I recommend the morning, mid-day, and in the evening before you go to bed. For the bedtime exercise, don't set an alarm (also, don't have your phone in your bedroom. If you use it for an alarm clock, stop!).

Burnout is not a failure on your part. You are a driven, giving person, and you want the best for others. Unfortunately, you've forgotten to take care of yourself first. I get it. I was the same way, then my 369 Days hit, and wow, did that cause a ripple effect.

CHAPTER 13
COVID-19

The majority of this book was written prior to March, 2020, when the global pandemic we know as COVID-19 was in full effect. Businesses across the world, and especially in North America, had to shut down immediately, to help "flatten the curve" (aka minimize the spread of this virus). Millions of people were suddenly quarantined in their homes, separated from loved ones and co-workers, and completely thrown off by what was happening.

I have to give credit to the countless organizations that were able to virtualize their offices and create remote working opportunities, preventing the need to furlough or lay off employees. Doing this helped reduce the strain on governments to pay unemployment wages to more people than we are already without work.

When people started working from home (#WFH), my initial thought was that this would be a golden opportunity for employees and employers to hit the pause button and reflect on the work pace they were maintaining prior to COVID-19. In every chapter before this one, I've highlighted that the way society was working was . . . well, not working. Burnout was an epidemic. The World Health Organization (WHO) has an ICD code for burnout, which in itself should be a huge warning, because the WHO doesn't issue ICD codes on a whim. My thought was that people could relax a little more, gain some time from not having to commute, and work at a slower pace.

I WAS WRONG.

NordVPN released a study in Spring 2020 on working hours. The study indicated that in the US, the average working day increased 40 percent, or three hours per day. People were working long hours prior to COVID-19, so add an additional three hours to the mix, and you are begging for burnout.

Why is this happening?

There are a plethora of reasons why people are working longer, and are suffering from #WFH burnout:

Homeschooling
Improper Work-From-Home Setup
Other People at Home
Video Meeting Fatigue
Bad Management
Worrying About the Future

Let's dive into each of these items.

HOMESCHOOLING

After the pandemic, many parents took on new full-time jobs as school teachers. While many school districts had online curriculum and the teachers were able to conduct some school activities virtually, most teachers were not teaching your children online all day. Thus, your role as a parent now included educating your children during your own work day. It was multitasking at its worst.

On social media, we all saw the memes and comments about parents wanting to expel their students or switch them to another class. It was funny, but it brought to light how important our education system is and how incredibly valuable our educators are. Sometime during the next school year (or whenever your kids are allowed to attend school in person), please, at minimum, buy your children's teachers some gift cards. I trust you realize how hard and important teachers' jobs are by now.

When you're tasked with educating your kids during the workday, doing it all is an insurmountable task. You can't do it. You've tried, I know, and failed miserably. I tell people all the time, you don't need to be giving an A+ effort right now to everything. You can't keep up with that pace and not burn out.

Strong employers understand the needs of their employees, and they should understand that many of their employees are teaching their children during the "normal" work day. Your company should scale back the work loads of every employee during this pandemic and only work on the critical things that serve your clients or customers. (More on that when I discuss bad management.)

IMPROPER WORK-FROM-HOME SETUP

There's a good chance that many of you reading this book never had the opportunity to work from home before. Your home may not have been set up for a home office, so when you were tossed into a #WFH scenario, you were not likely prepared. In the early days of the pandemic, it was challenging to acquire the necessary tools for working remotely (chairs, desks, office supplies, etc.), so it was a stressful time for many. I advise people to set up their remote working environments as effectively as they can. It's essential to consider ergonomics, since access to massage therapy is limited during a pandemic! Don't work in your bed. Your bed is meant for other things, and work shouldn't be one of them. Also get your employer to supply your equipment needs. It shouldn't be the employee's responsibility to foot the bill for the big items like computers, printers, chairs, and desks. If your employer can't (or won't) do this, then keep your receipts and write off the expenses on next year's taxes.

OTHER PEOPLE AT HOME

Working at home can be a challenge for those who haven't done it before, and it's a real challenge if your spouse, partner, or roommate is also there. Most homes only have one area that could be deemed a "work area," so when you have multiple people at home all day (and night), it gets stressful.

A great colleague of mine who's a divorce attorney has seen a significant spike in divorce cases during this pandemic. Apparently spending too much time with people brings out their true colors. The prolonged stress of working side- by- side with your housemate builds up, even in the strongest of relationships. The key is to communicate your needs with your housemates and children, and set specific times when you can be interrupted. Soundproof headphones are a great option for this! When the headphones are on, it should be like a Do Not Disturb sign.

Video Meeting Fatigue

Organizations that went virtual decided to use video conferencing to communicate with their employees. The issue I've seen is that there are way too many meetings. This was also the case before COVID-19, but it's gotten worse during the pandemic. Some organizations require the video call stay active during the work day so managers can "easily see" (aka spy) on their workers to make sure they're working and not watching Netflix.

(FYI: From this point forward, when I use the term " Zoom," I'm referring to any type of video calling, such as Skype, Hangouts, or Facetime.)

If there was ever a time for a revolution in how employees are treated in the workplace, now is that time. Strong companies compensate their employees by deliverables, not how much time they spend on a Zoom call. Give your employees their tasks and be available if they have questions, but then get the heck out of their way and let them do their job.

The Zoom fatigue is real. Companies are having calls multiple times during the day, night, and even on weekends. If that was the norm for you prior to COVID-19, you should've updated your Resume.doc long ago and got the heck out of that crappy organization. You still can. New opportunities still exist. My better half interviewed and was hired for a new role during the pandemic. Don't listen to the naysayers. There are opportunities out there. Go find them.

BAD MANAGEMENT

I co-wrote a whole book on bad management called *Pre-Emptive Strike Leadership*, so I won't rewrite what's written in that book, other than to highlight that the reason your company has dozens of Zoom calls every week is that you have bad management. The managers don't trust you to do your job. Why? Because those managers lack the skills and self-confidence to step back to let you do the work once they've assigned it to you. They may also be control freaks or narcissists who want to control every step you take.

Bad managers who require their teams to be on Zoom calls all day, every day are burning out their teams. Great managers will be available for check-ins, but they don't meet for the sake of meeting. We don't need to create virtual participation ribbons for meetings that should've been emails.

WORRYING ABOUT THE FUTURE

Many of us have anxiety about how this pandemic will unfold. When our lives dramatically change in an instant, it's amazing how much it can impact our mental state. Restaurants, bars, movie theaters, and going to work all stopped in March, 2020, and at the time of writing (Summer, 2020), some things are still closed. It's only been a few months since things closed, but it feels much longer.

For those who are not working right now, finances are a huge concern. During my 369 days of worst-case scenarios back in 2009- 10, I experienced significant financial challenges that led to my losing the family car and home. This pandemic actually triggered me with some past trauma from that period of time. I was in a funk in early April for a couple days and couldn't grasp why I was feeling the way I was. After watching some news coverage of long lines for people to get a couple bags of groceries, I realized why. My empathy was bleeding into past traumatic thoughts.

These thoughts were not real in the present, but they were quite real in the past. Thankfully, I was able to rebound and recognize what was happening, and I did the self-care work (journaling, meditation, etc.) that helped bring me back to my reality. I'm immensely grateful that my life is better now, and I want everyone to be free from burnout, no matter what's going on in the world.

How To Avoid #WFH Burnout

Throughout this book, I've provided examples of how to prevent burnout from happening or how to recover from it if it's already happened to you—but in case you skipped right to this chapter, I'll summarize those tips.

Get restful sleep.
Turn off unnecessary notifications on your smartphone.
Eat healthier.
Be active.
Set time boundaries around when you start work, and when you end your work day.
Journal and meditate.
Work on your bucket list.

Of the above items, setting time boundaries around your working hours is critical in preventing burnout. Adding an additional three hours to your workday is not good for your mental or physical health, especially in light of everything else going on in the world.

CHAPTER 14
CLOSING THOUGHTS

We've covered a lot of ground in this book. I trust that you have some enlightenment on what burnout is, what its causes are, and some techniques to help you recover from burnout. More importantly, you've learned skills to prevent burnout from happening to you again. Burnout is something that can come back. I hear countless stories about how people have been burned out on numerous occasions. Once is bad enough.

In closing, I'll share my experience from a couple years ago that was leading me down the path to the dark side of burnout. My summer had been busy, and I recognized that it was beginning to take a toll on my well-being. (Burnout can sneak up on you, even if you are a thought leader in that subject.) I was doing quite a bit of travelling, attending conferences, recording podcasts, co-writing a book, writing articles, and so forth. I was triaging my calendar (eating my own dog food, as they say in I.T.), and recognized that my fall of that year had a ton of travel and a heavy recording schedule for my podcast show.

I decided to drop a grenade in my fall schedule and build in more time off from my show. I scheduled more time off than I normally need, because I recognized I needed more time. I had been so busy with my passion for work, that it started taking a toll. Thankfully, I knew the warning signs and acted accordingly. You can do that too. It's your life and your schedule.

BreakfastLeadership.com/Resources has free resources that can help you on your journey. I am a certified Cognitive Behavioral Therapist and certified Neuro Linguistic Practitioner, and I work with teams and individuals on burnout recovery and prevention, and workplace culture. Go to BreakfastLeadership.com/hire-us to schedule a no-obligation call.

Please email Support@BreakfastLeadership.com if you have specific questions about burnout or this book.

I show organizations and individuals how to burnout-proof their lives. If your company (or yourself) is facing burnout, get help ASAP.

Here's where to find me on social media:

My talk on Smartphone addiction and burnout: http://bit.ly/BLiBinky
LinkedIn: https://www.linkedin.com/in/bfastleadership/
Twitter: https://twitter.com/bfastleadership
Facebook: https://www.facebook.com/bfastleadership/
Instagram: https://www.instagram.com/bfastleadership/
YouTube: http://bit.ly/BkfastYouTube

The Breakfast Leadership App is available on The App Store and Google Play.

Be well!

www.ingramcontent.com/pod-product-compliance
Lightning Source LLC
Chambersburg PA
CBHW051816050726
47598CB00006B/2584